Psalm 116
A 30-day Devotional on Rescue, Redemption and the Life We Live in Response

For Jacob
Thank you for introducing me to Jesus,
David Wilcox, and Paul Hewson

‖ Table of Contents ‖

‖ INTRODUCTION ‖

Psalm 116

1 I love the Lord, for he heard my voice; he heard my cry for mercy. **2** Because he turned his ear to me, I will call on him as long as I live. **3** The cords of death entangled me, the anguish of the grave came over me; I was overcome by distress and sorrow. **4** Then I called on the name of the Lord: "Lord, save me!" **5** The Lord is gracious and righteous; our God is full of compassion **6** The Lord protects the unwary; when I was brought low, he saved me. **7** Return to your rest, my soul, for the Lord has been good to you. **8** For you, Lord, have delivered me from death, my eyes from tears, my feet from stumbling, **9** that I may walk before the Lord in the land of the living. **10** I trusted in the Lord when I said, "I am greatly afflicted"; **11** in my alarm I said, "Everyone is a liar." **12** What shall I return to the Lord for all his goodness to me? **13** I will lift up the cup of salvation and call on the name of the Lord. **14** I will fulfill my vows to the Lord in the presence of all his people. **15** Precious in the sight of the Lord is the death of his faithful servants. **16** Truly I am your servant, Lord; I serve you just as my mother did; you have freed me from my chains. **17** I will sacrifice a thank offering to you and call on the name of the Lord. **18** I will fulfill my vows to the Lord in the presence of all his people, **19** in the courts of the house of the Lord - in your midst, Jerusalem. Praise the Lord.

The richness of the psalms, as a collection, is in their breadth. There are songs of pure praise and the lamentations of deeply troubled souls. The language is visceral and the experiences are universal to the human race, allowing the psalms to become more than wisdom or history. They take on an almost-interactive quality, an identifiable beauty and commonality for all who have walked this earth.

In Psalm 116, David recalls a troubling season of life, where sorrow overshadowed salvation and death seemed much closer than deliverance. In recounting God's rescue and redemption in his life, David then pivots to praising God. He seeks a way to live his life as a thank offering to God for the graciousness and deep blessing he had received.

We, too, face troubling seasons, deep trials, and moments of acute crisis. And we have also been rescued and redeemed through the gracious work of Jesus Christ. As we remember our own seasons of struggle, we can be encouraged that we are never alone. Then, like David, we can ask the question of how we might live in response to the incredible blessing we have in Jesus.

This month-long devotional intends to bring us to a place of remembrance of our own rescue by God so that we might be launched into a life that is a worthy response to His gift.

My prayer is that Psalm 116 will find us becoming reacquainted with our trials, reminded of our blessings, and recommitted to living the life we're called to as children of God.

II

As a 30-day devotional, the design of this work is to provide a pathway to walk along with David as he traces God's rescue and redemption in his life and measures out what his response should be.

The psalm is broken down into 5 parts, each with a six-day emphasis. Psalm 116 is a movement, a sort of symphonic procession through something that is universal among believers in the God of the Bible. This devotional will lead us through that procession, enduring Sorrow to Salvation (v1-4), enjoying God's Perfect Protection (v5-7), savoring Rescue and Redemption (v8-11), diving into the Response to Blessing (v12-14), and finishing by examining the Life to Give (v15-19).

At the beginning of each of these 5 parts, there is a brief overview of the corresponding text (which is set in context of the larger psalm) as a means of setting the heart for the 6 days that will follow.

The devotional closes with Psalm 116 laid out again in full. This is our reminder that this is not a collection of pithy thoughts and ideas, but a larger work to be appreciated in its fullness. We are, in a sense, sitting at a feast. We may slice it into parts so we can ingest and enjoy it, but being able to sit back and see the whole table allow us to truly appreciate and savor the life-giving nourishment on offer for our souls.

Psalm 116 is beautiful. It is resonant. It is ours to cherish deeply. Enjoy.

II SORROW TO SALVATION II

Week 1: Psalm 116:1-4

1 I love the Lord, for he heard my voice;
he heard my cry for mercy.
2 Because he turned his ear to me,
I will call on him as long as I live.
3 The cords of death entangled me,
the anguish of the grave came over me;
I was overcome by distress and sorrow.
4 Then I called on the name of the Lord:
"Lord, save me!"

Jesus was asked about which of the commandments was the greatest. Rather than invent a new command, He rested on the wisdom of Deuteronomy 6, the *shema*, with its imploring of the faithful to "Love the Lord your God with all your heart and with all your soul and with all your strength."

David, having been through deep trials, overcome by distress and sorrow, fulfills this command to love the Lord. Indeed, as is rarely done in Scripture, he directly and personally - as a child to a parent - declares his love for God. He is enraptured by God's goodness and attentiveness. The episode prompts David to declare a lifetime of future faithfulness as a result of God's inclined ear.

When David called on the name of the Lord, "Lord save me!", God listened and *heard.* This verb, in the original language, includes not just simple hearing but *answering* in its meaning. We see, then, that when David called out, God listened and intervened, bringing mercy and life to David so that he might overcome the cords of death in which he was entangled.

Day 1

Psalm 116:1-4

1 I love the Lord, for he heard my voice;
    he heard my cry for mercy.
2 Because he turned his ear to me,
    I will call on him as long as I live.
3 The cords of death entangled me,
    the anguish of the grave came over me;
    I was overcome by distress and sorrow.
4 Then I called on the name of the Lord:
    "Lord, save me!"

ANSWERING SPEECH *I love the Lord*, the psalmist declares. It is a responsive love to God's loving act of listening. God hears the psalmist's voice crying out, hears his pleas for mercy. Eugene Peterson declares that "all speech is answering speech", as God spoke the world into being. Our prayers are, then, simply a response to His speaking life into our lives, to God's willingness to speak *us* into being. This is an incredible truth. We have a God who not only initiated creation itself, but stays in intimate contact with the created man. When we cry out, we are heard by a just and merciful God.

Prayer: Father, I long for a spirit of humility. I am so quick to think that I am the author of my days, that I am in control of my life. Forgive my pride and remind me that my prayers, the deepest rumblings of my soul, are simply "answering speech", a response to you. Give me eyes to see your creation and, in it, your majesty, providence, and sovereignty. Amen.

Day 2

Psalm 116:1-4

1 I love the Lord, for he heard my voice;
    he heard my cry for mercy.
2 Because he turned his ear to me,
    I will call on him as long as I live.
3 The cords of death entangled me,
    the anguish of the grave came over me;
    I was overcome by distress and sorrow.
4 Then I called on the name of the Lord:
    "Lord, save me!"

THE ULTIMATE ANSWER In the midst of great danger, the David cries out to God. In his most desperate moments, he turns to the Lord. Over and over in Scripture, when the faithful come upon trials, they turn their eyes to heaven, the voices to the Creator. Even Jesus appealed to God to take the cup of suffering from Him in His time of greatest anguish in Gethsemane (Luke 22:42). Rather than receiving salvation, though, Jesus laid His life down and became salvation for all of mankind. Jesus became God's ultimate answer to our beleaguered cries.

Prayer: Lord, I confess that I too often look to you as a last resort. I seek to be my own savior when trouble comes long before I cry out to you. Remind me that what has been done in Jesus means that salvation has already come, that I am already secured in you. Find me close, Father, as I cling to the hope of your promises as the deliverance from my every trial. Amen.

Day 3

Psalm 116:1-4

1 I love the Lord, for he heard my voice;
   he heard my cry for mercy.
2 Because he turned his ear to me,
   I will call on him as long as I live.
3 The cords of death entangled me,
   the anguish of the grave came over me;
   I was overcome by distress and sorrow.
4 Then I called on the name of the Lord:
   "Lord, save me!"

BORN BOUND The Hebrew behind the entangling cords (verse 3) signifies a binding, potentially alluding to the custom of binding victims for slaughter or criminals on their way to execution. This is the depth of trouble the psalmist is in the midst of which leads him to *the anguish of the grave*. Such trouble is an inevitability in this life, as we are all born bound by sin and on our way to certain death. If not for the willingness of Christ to be bound on the cross on our behalf, the cords of death would have had their victory over us. Alas, by his wounds we are healed and set free (Isaiah 53:5).

Prayer: Heavenly Father, remind me again of the cost of my life. Remind my heart that I have not earned my salvation, but that Jesus paid the ultimate price to see me set free. Father, I long to have a heart that is centered on this truth and a life that is a clear a response to it - an undeniable witness based in gratitude to you. Thank you for saving me. May I live it out anew today. Amen.

Day 4

Psalm 116:1-4

1 I love the Lord, for he heard my voice;
    he heard my cry for mercy.
2 Because he turned his ear to me,
    I will call on him as long as I live.
3 The cords of death entangled me,
    the anguish of the grave came over me;
    I was overcome by distress and sorrow.
4 Then I called on the name of the Lord:
    "Lord, save me!"

INCLINED David is clear in understanding his cry was heard by the Lord because God had turned His ear toward man. Another translation says the Lord *inclined His ear* towards the psalmist. We are grateful for a God who will take a posture that says "I'm listening" even as we so often fail to do the same. We incline our ears towards every outlet in culture, hoping for wisdom, relief, excitement, and security. God heard our cries and inclined His ear - and His Son - to us. To what other source would we rather incline our hearts and minds?

Prayer: Lord, I have turned my ear away from you. I am inclined to read the news, scroll through the online statuses of those only tangentially connected to me, and otherwise look for hope - or at least distraction - in every source but you. Father, I know that you alone deserve my attention, my inclined heart and mind. Help me to see that every day, to grow in trusting you alone to satisfy me. Amen.

Day 5

Psalm 116:1-4

1 I love the Lord, for he heard my voice;
    he heard my cry for mercy.
2 Because he turned his ear to me,
    I will call on him as long as I live.
3 The cords of death entangled me,
    the anguish of the grave came over me;
    I was overcome by distress and sorrow.
4 Then I called on the name of the Lord:
    "Lord, save me!"

OVERCOME There are few sensations a unforgettable as the experience of wading out into the ocean only to be consumed, to be overcome, by a breaking wave. The feeling can be surprising and frightening. The psalmist is overcome by distress and sorrow, as the roiling white waters of the *anguish of the grave* swallowed him. Completely overwhelmed by the circumstances of life, David cries out, calling on the name of the Lord. When we find ourselves tossed about by the waves of life, overcome by grief or despondency or resentment, do we furiously paddle in an effort to save ourselves or do we cry out for the rescuer who created the wind and the waves and commands them with a single word (Mark 4:39)?

Prayer: Heavenly Father, I am so easily overcome. I find myself awash in my own emotions and circumstances far more often than my pride would like to admit. Remind me, Lord, that you command the earth and the heavens. Remind me that you still the seas and can still the storms of my life. Forgive my worry and anxiety and remind me that nothing that comes upon me is a surprise to you. Guide me through the waves. Amen.

Day 6

Psalm 116:1-4

1 I love the Lord, for he heard my voice;
   he heard my cry for mercy.
2 Because he turned his ear to me,
   I will call on him as long as I live.
3 The cords of death entangled me,
   the anguish of the grave came over me;
   I was overcome by distress and sorrow.
4 Then I called on the name of the Lord:
   "Lord, save me!"

NOTHING LESS *"Lord, save me!"* These words are a desperate cry. There are no shortage of false saviors on offer to humanity. We chase salvation in new technology and new philosophy. We seek saviors in unhealthy relationships and in modern humanism, the worship of man's ability to act as gods of our own destiny. None of these replacements satisfy and none fill us with the significance they promise. Technology becomes obsolete. Philosophies are updated. Relationships crumble under the weight of unrealistic pressure. Leaders and human efforts always fall short of perfection. Only God will satisfy, secure, and save us.

Prayer: Father, I call on your name today. I am weary of the failures of this life, from the never-ending news stream of daily destruction.I am exhausted by my own inability to stay on the path you've called me to walk. You have saved me already through Jesus; find me faithful, calling on your name as long as I live. Amen.

‖ PERFECT PROTECTION ‖

Week 2: Psalm 116:5-7

5 The Lord is gracious and righteous;
  our God is full of compassion.
6 The Lord protects the unwary;
  when I was brought low, he saved me.
7 Return to your rest, my soul,
  for the Lord has been good to you.

We all hold internal conversations as we go about our lives, an oft-critical play-by-play of our existence in this world. Psychologists call this "self-talk" and, increasingly, say that whether it is constructive or destructive has a legitimate impact on the outcome of our days.

Throughout the psalms, David practices a different kind of talk, an ongoing affirmation and remembrance of who God is and what He has done. In times of distress, God's rescue is remembered. In times of sorrow, God's comfort is considered.

The repeated imploring of Scripture is "Re-member!" Remember your chains. And then consider how you've been set free. Remember your bonds. And then be humbled at how God has loosed them. Remember your rescue. And then marvel at the love of Christ to take on the cross. Remember your redemption. And then bask in the rays of a God-given purpose to celebrate God and participate in the restoration of this earth.

Return to your rest, my soul. The Lord has been very, very good to you.

Day 7

Psalm 116:5-7

5 The Lord is gracious and righteous;
  our God is full of compassion.
6 The Lord protects the unwary;
  when I was brought low, he saved me.
7 Return to your rest, my soul,
  for the Lord has been good to you.

RELYING ON TRUTH In seasons of trial, it is essential to recall what is true rather than what feels true in the moment. While fasting in the desert, Jesus is approached and tempted by the devil (Matthew 4:1-11). We can only imagine the emotional, physical, and spiritual exhaustion that might come with a lack of nourishment in such extreme conditions. Jesus is not swayed by his emotions or momentary need but, rather, relies on the truth of Scripture to combat the temptation of the evil one. The psalmist, having faced death and anguish, similarly recalls the graciousness and goodness of God as comfort in the storm.

Prayer: Lord, I praise you for who you are and how you have broken through the darkness to give me light. In seasons when the darkness threatens to return, find your word on my lips. Help me recall your goodness and remind my heart of the depth of your love that rescued me once and for all eternity. Amen.

Day 8

Psalm 116:5-7

5 The Lord is gracious and righteous;
  our God is full of compassion.
6 The Lord protects the unwary;
  when I was brought low, he saved me.
7 Return to your rest, my soul,
  for the Lord has been good to you.

SIMPLE PROTECTION The psalmist declares that "The Lord protects the unwary." Other translations use the word *simple* rather than *unwary.* This is the picture of an unwitting tourist who is vulnerable to pickpockets and scam artists due to ignorance or naïveté. We tend to think of ourselves as sophisticated individuals in our post-modern society. The Scripture, however, paints a different picture, using words like weak, powerless, and helpless (Romans 5:6). David, in his humility, recognizes this standing before the Lord and praises God for protecting those who cannot protect themselves and, ultimately, for saving those who cannot save themselves.

Prayer: Lord, let me not be swayed by the lies I have believed. No technology or education or self-actualization can save me, much less protect me, from the pain and heartache of a broken world. Let me see myself as you see me, lost and vulnerable and in desperate need. Then, Father, let me boldly walk the path you've made for me in Jesus, humbly living out my days as your adopted child. Amen.

Day 9

Psalm 116:5-7

5 The Lord is gracious and righteous;
 our God is full of compassion.
6 The Lord protects the unwary;
 when I was brought low, he saved me.
7 Return to your rest, my soul,
 for the Lord has been good to you.

INTO THE DEPTHS Our society has a great aversion to trial and pain. Though it is inevitable, we instinctively run from suffering. And yet, once in the midst of a trial, we so often see God work to heal, restore, and renew. The psalmist recognizes that he was saved from a *low* place. He is not alone. Consider the words of Jonah in his lowest hour: *From deep in the realm of the dead I called for help, and you listened to my cry.* (Jonah 2:2) This life promises difficult times, low seasons, and deep hurt. We have a God who intends to work all of these things out for the good of those who love Him (Romans 8:28). Call on His name.

Prayer: Father, I confess to being surprised when seasons of tragedy or trial come upon me. Lord, let me be prepared for the rigors of this life and let me remain watchful with your name on my lips. In my low seasons, deliver from the temptation of false saviors and quick fixes and find me crying out to you alone for rescue and redemption. Amen.

Day 10

Psalm 116:5-7

5 The Lord is gracious and righteous;
  our God is full of compassion.
6 The Lord protects the unwary;
  when I was brought low, he saved me.
7 Return to your rest, my soul,
  for the Lord has been good to you.

TRUE REST David, having been rescued from his trial, addresses his own soul and tells it to *return* to rest. Scripture teaches that God has set eternity in the human heart (Ecclesiastes 3:11), some remembrance of what life was like at rest (the Hebrew *sabat*) in the His presence. For followers of Jesus, there is true rest available. This rest is not in finding our way out of a season of trouble but in finding our way into the saving grace of Jesus. Jesus is the true *sabbath*, as we are able to cease working for our own salvation and bask in His glorious, saving, and eternal work. Not only is Jesus "Lord of the Sabbath" (Matthew 12:8), but, for those who in him, He is our true sabbath, our eternal rest.

Prayer: Gracious Father, find me at rest in you. I spend too many days working to earn the salvation you freely gave me and hustling to become significant in the eyes of those around me. Remind my soul that my salvation is in you and that my identity in you is my only lasting significance. Find me at rest in you alone, Lord. Amen.

Day 11

Psalm 116:5-7

5 The Lord is gracious and righteous;
   our God is full of compassion.
6 The Lord protects the unwary;
   when I was brought low, he saved me.
7 Return to your rest, my soul,
   for the Lord has been good to you.

FAMILIAR SUFFERING Seasons of trial
and suffering can be isolating in our culture
as we fail to find others who can truly empathize with what we are going through. In
Jesus, God sent a savior who would not
only accomplish the work of redeeming us,
but would also walk among people so as to
be able to empathize with our weaknesses
and temptations (Hebrews 4:15). Jesus was
a man of suffering, familiar with pain (Isaiah
53:3) and this truth should comfort us. We
don't cry out to a distant, impersonal entity,
but to an intimate savior who knows our
heartache and frailty.

Prayer: Father God, thank you for the way
you saved me. I too often paint you as an
impersonal spiritual being who can't fully

know what I am going through. Restore the truth in my heart that you know my suffering and experienced a greater suffering. You know my pain and experienced a greater pain. You chose to know my weakness so I could share in your glorious, saving strength. Gladden my heart at the thought, O Lord. I am known and highly favored. Amen.

Day 12

Psalm 116:5-7

5 The Lord is gracious and righteous;
　　our God is full of compassion.
6 The Lord protects the unwary;
　　when I was brought low, he saved me.
7 Return to your rest, my soul,
　　for the Lord has been good to you.

THINK ON THESE THINGS When the apostle Paul wrote to the Philippians, he addressed the way to having a peace that transcends all understanding. In addition to prescribing ongoing Christian practices, Paul urged his readers to think about that which is true, noble, right, pure, lovely, and admirable. In this, he said, the God of peace will be with you (Philippians 4:7-9). Paul's charge is reminiscent of the psalmist's practice in Psalm 116. In seeking to lead his soul back to rest, David recounts both the righteous and restorative actions of God and the unwavering attributes of God. Such remembrances remind us that a good and just God is not only involved in our lives, but in control of our eternity.

Prayer: Lord, I pray you would *bind my wandering heart to thee.* My mind seeks cheap entertainment and my heart looks for instant (if shallow) gratification. Let me rest deeply in truth instead - find me thinking on all that you are and all that you've done. I trust you with my eternity, Lord. Let me surrender not only my days, but my every thought as well. Amen.

‖ RESCUE AND REDEMP-
TION ‖

Week 3: Psalm 116:8-11

8 For you, Lord, have delivered me from
death,
    my eyes from tears,
    my feet from stumbling,
9 that I may walk before the Lord
    in the land of the living.
10 I trusted in the Lord when I said,
    "I am greatly afflicted";
11 in my alarm I said,
    "Everyone is a liar."

A reality of life that we all come to grips
with at some point is that there is not a
question as to whether we'll go through
various storms. Rather, there is only a
question of when and how severe those
storms will be.

David recognizes his deliverance while jux-
taposing his reliance on humanity and his
trust in the Lord. The state of a fallen world
means that the battles of a believer are not
only supernatural, but often interpersonal.
People fail us. We fail others. Our imperfec-

tion leads to all sorts of conflict that can create a sense of hopelessness about our fellow travelers on this journey.

When David threw his hands in the air while declaring that no one was trustworthy, he did it on the back of another statement. The Lord delivered him, dried his tears, and made clear his path. While people may fail us, the Lord is worthy of our total trust.

Day 13

Psalm 116:8-11

8 For you, Lord, have delivered me from death,
    my eyes from tears,
    my feet from stumbling,
9 that I may walk before the Lord
    in the land of the living.
10 I trusted in the Lord when I said,
    "I am greatly afflicted";
11 in my alarm I said,
    "Everyone is a liar."

DELIVERED FROM DEATH David recognizes that *the cords of death entangled* him (v 3) and that rescue from death was the Lord's doing. We often forget our own complicity in our trouble. Like Job, we assert our innocence and rest in a victim mentality. But God, aware of our failings, still chooses to bring back our souls from the pit of emptiness and enlighten us with the light of life (Job 33). Whether in choosing evil or choosing simply to trust in something other than God, we become stuck in the muck and mire that sin brings. Thankfully, we have a Savior who saves us not based on our merit or faithfulness. Rather, Jesus comes to our rescue because of His great love for us.

Prayer: Father, illuminate my heart and mind. Show me the places that I am walking willfully away from you and into danger. Thank you for chasing me down the paths of death I chose and for gently guiding me back towards the way of life. I long to be a witness to your rescue. Find your grace on my lips and your love evident in my life. Amen.

Day 14

Psalm 116:8-11

8 For you, Lord, have delivered me from death,
    my eyes from tears,
    my feet from stumbling,
9 that I may walk before the Lord
    in the land of the living.
10 I trusted in the Lord when I said,
    "I am greatly afflicted";
11 in my alarm I said,
    "Everyone is a liar."

FARTHER KINDNESS It is something remarkable to be delivered from death. Stories of heroic rescue from the precipice are fodder for epic novels and grandiose films. And yet, how much sweeter is the picture laid out by the psalmist? To quote Calvin, "God has not only rescued me from present death, but also treated me with farther kindness, in chasing away sorrow, and stretching out His hand to prevent me from stumbling." Not only were we once dead in our transgressions, but we've been restored to fullness of life (Ephesians 2:4-9). This is amazing grace.

Prayer: Lord, your love is extravagant. And still, I confess to looking to the world to find some shred of significance and experience some shadow of the fullness I've known in you. I know that my true significance is in your willingness to adopt me and call me your child. I know fullness is found in you alone. I long to rest in your extravagant love. May I know your embrace afresh today. Amen.

Day 15

Psalm 116:8-11

8 For you, Lord, have delivered me from
death,
    my eyes from tears,
    my feet from stumbling,
9 that I may walk before the Lord
    in the land of the living.
10 I trusted in the Lord when I said,
    "I am greatly afflicted";
11 in my alarm I said,
    "Everyone is a liar."

PRESENT LIFE What is it to *walk before
the Lord*? It is to live in the presence of
God, under His charge. Once almost dead,
this *land of the living* is now a place of safe-
ty, under the watchful eye of the Father. It is
seeing life from such a perspective that
gives David such confidence and joy.
Where we were once drowning in sin and
darkness, vulnerable to the death of the
deep, we now find security in holding tightly
to the preserver of our lives. Our rescuer,
Jesus, did not shout instructions to His beleaguered people as our noses dipped under the waterline. Instead, He jumped into

the churning water with us and rescued us by taking for Himself the death that was designed for us. In Him, we truly live this present life.

Prayer: Lord, there are days that I find myself drowning in the very waters from which you have already rescued me. I return to my sin, only to cry out again for your hand to swing down low to drag me to the shore and show me the path to life. Forgive me where I've taken this life for granted. Forgive me where I've walked right back into brokenness. Heal me again, Lord, and lead me away from temptation. Amen.

Day 16

Psalm 116:8-11

8 For you, Lord, have delivered me from death,
    my eyes from tears,
    my feet from stumbling,
9 that I may walk before the Lord
    in the land of the living.
10 I trusted in the Lord when I said,
    "I am greatly afflicted";
11 in my alarm I said,
    "Everyone is a liar."

BELIEF MANIFESTED To believe is a powerful thing. To believe and, therefore, act is an evidence of something far greater. The apostle Paul quotes the psalmist when writing to the church at Corinth, encouraging them not to lose heart (2 Corinthians 4:13). If we trust the Lord, we can walk with confidence in the midst of the greatest storms. As Paul further explains, this light momentary affliction is preparing us for an eternal weight of glory. (2 Corinthians 4:17) There is a profound beauty when belief in the unseen things of God is made manifest through lives that prove faithful in the face of even the harshest trials of the seen world.

Prayer: Dear God, I believe. Help me, yet, where my belief is weak, where my belief has not made it from my heart to my hands. Let me be a vessel not of private faith but of public virtue for your glory. May I be so secure in your love that I can recklessly love all of those around me, regardless of their class, belief, orientation, persuasion, or status.

Day 17

Psalm 116:8-11

8 For you, Lord, have delivered me from
death,
    my eyes from tears,
    my feet from stumbling,
9 that I may walk before the Lord
    in the land of the living.
10 I trusted in the Lord when I said,
    "I am greatly afflicted";
11 in my alarm I said,
    "Everyone is a liar."

TRUST IN THE STORM No person makes
it through life without being let down by another. Nobody escapes feeling alone and
abandoned in the midst of trials and affliction. David is no exception. In lamenting
that *everyone is a liar*, he has laid bare his
heart. He feels utterly alone, as if there is
no one left who can help him through the
storm. The disciples once felt that way,
wondering aloud if Jesus even cared
whether they lived or died as waves began
to sink the boat in which they traveled. Jesus, unshaken, commanded the storm to be
still and the wind and waves instantly

obeyed him (Mark 4:35-41). It is a frightening experience to find ourselves with no one to trust, with life seemingly slipping away. In life's difficult days, we must remember that Jesus was abandoned on the cross so that we would never again be alone in this life. Call on Him, as God alone can calm the storms of this life.

Prayer: Father, I am so forgetful. You are faithful to remind me, though - you are the only one who brings me peace. In my darkest hour, when I was drowning in the storm of sin, you reached down and rescued me. Lord, you didn't delay my death or suspend my punishment. You eliminated my death and replaced it with life. You erased my debt and have shown me a future of hopefulness and peace. Find me trusting you more as I remember your goodness. Amen.

Day 18

Psalm 116:8-11

8 For you, Lord, have delivered me from death,
    my eyes from tears,
    my feet from stumbling,
9 that I may walk before the Lord
    in the land of the living.
10 I trusted in the Lord when I said,
    "I am greatly afflicted";
11 in my alarm I said,
    "Everyone is a liar."

LIGHTER THAN BREATH It is tempting to see worldly success and desire it above the things of God. We are all witness to the highlight reels of others' life through any number of mediums. The only struggles we can see, though, typically belong to us. But success and status in this world are *lighter than breath*, fleeting vanity that cannot sustain our deepest hopes (Psalm 62:9-10). Success in this world may yet come to us. God may see fit to increase our influence or our affluence. The warning of Scripture is clear - do not set your heart upon these things. Only God is eternal. Only God is lasting. He has delivered us. As we clear the tears from our eyes, may we see with His eternal perspective.

Prayer: Lord, I aim so much of my life towards the waypoint of worldly success. I confess that I too often yearn for the applause of men much more than I desire you. Help me to see my days and my strivings as lighter than breath and to see you as the weighty, glorious pursuit of my days. Give me the view from your eyes. Amen.

II RESPONSE TO BLESS-ING II

Week 4: Psalm 116:12-14

12 What shall I return to the Lord
    for all his goodness to me?
13 I will lift up the cup of salvation
    and call on the name of the Lord.
14 I will fulfill my vows to the Lord
    in the presence of all his people.

Gratitude comes in many forms, although it usually follows a simple rule: the greater the gift, the greater the gratitude. Many gifts inspire us to write words of thanks. Rarer still are gifts that require something more in return.

Imagine the greatness of a gift that could inspire the receiver to offer his own life in gratitude. In a very real sense, David looks upon the goodness of the Lord and decides that it will require something truly special to convey his thankfulness. No words, however beautiful, will accomplish what is in his soul to communicate.

He takes the posture of a man in immense debt, vowing to live out his days as an offering back to the Lord. Having been spared and rescued and blessed beyond imagination, David knows no other fitting reply than to give his very life. The greater the gift...

Day 19

Psalm 116:12-14

12 What shall I return to the Lord
    for all his goodness to me?
13 I will lift up the cup of salvation
    and call on the name of the Lord.
14 I will fulfill my vows to the Lord
    in the presence of all his people.

STREAM OF ETERNITY Every moment of our lives is a response. We enter a world that was established long before us. We join a society shaped by those who predate us. We serve a God who knew us before the foundation of the earth, who had plans for us before we entered our mother's wombs (Jeremiah 1:4-5). All of our lives is, then, a response. The psalmist rightly asks what he might return to God, what he might give back in using this life that was first given to him. This is a profound concept and it requires us to suspend our me-centric worldview long enough to gain a proper perspective. We enter into the stream of eternity for only a brief moment. What will our response be?

PRAYER Heavenly Father, forgive me for making this life about me. You breathed me into being, laid a path before my feet, and saved me in Jesus long before I ever knew I was in need of rescue. Lord, open my eyes to the reality of your eternity. Let me see as you do for a moment, that I might live a life that is a worthy response to your grace. Amen.

Day 20

Psalm 116:12-14

12 What shall I return to the Lord
   for all his goodness to me?
13 I will lift up the cup of salvation
   and call on the name of the Lord.
14 I will fulfill my vows to the Lord
   in the presence of all his people.

ALL HIS GOODNESS David asks what he might return to God for the immense goodness that has been poured out upon his life. Before we can even get to an answer to the psalmist's question, we would be wise to consider *all his goodness*. We, as a people, are generally terrible with gratitude. We seek one surface-level satisfaction after another and we find ourselves in a cycle of unfulfilled desire. To stop and consider the breadth and depth of God's goodness is to be stunned into silent gratitude. Consider His design and His salvation. Consider all of the beauty in between - relationships and love, childbirth and laughter, sunrises and hope. To truly ponder the goodness of God is to know true gratitude.

PRAYER God, I am a fickle creature. I find myself more interested in shiny trinkets and slick marketing than in your unknowably vast design of the universe or the unfathomably intricate design of humanity itself. Stop me in my tracks, Lord. Show me your beauty again. Let me appreciate love and laughter anew. And let me be found so deeply grateful as I share your beauty and justice with those around me. Amen.

Day 21

Psalm 116:12-14

12 What shall I return to the Lord
   for all his goodness to me?
13 I will lift up the cup of salvation
   and call on the name of the Lord.
14 I will fulfill my vows to the Lord
   in the presence of all his people.

A TOAST TO GOD Having had an abundance of blessing poured out upon his life, David vows to return in kind - to pour out his life as an offering in response. Eugene Peterson's translation of this passage in *The Message* captures the beauty of this concept saying, "I'll lift high the cup of salvation—a toast to God!" This is the essence of David's vow - to lift high the cup of salvation is to live a life as a toast to the Almighty, reminiscent of the drink offering called for in the time of Moses (Numbers 28:7). What a perfect picture! Glasses in the air, our days are lived as inspiration, hope, and anticipation are made manifest at the celebration feast of life.

PRAYER Lord, thank you for the blessings you've poured out on me. Thank you for life and love, for the redemption of your rescue. May my life honor you in response. I pray that I would live out my days in such a way that others would see not only the offering I present, but the celebration at which I present it. Find me celebrating your goodness and grace every day, regardless of season or circumstance. I long to lift high the cup of salvation to you, Lord. Amen.

Day 22

Psalm 116:12-14

12 What shall I return to the Lord
for all his goodness to me?
13 I will lift up the cup of salvation
and call on the name of the Lord.
14 I will fulfill my vows to the Lord
in the presence of all his people.

FAITHFUL NOT FAMOUS Our world is one of celebrity and fame. We spend countless hours cheering on heroes in the world of sports and following the beautiful population of the big screen. We have even cultivated our own little acreage of celebrity in social media. Here, people can like and affirm our personal posts and photos, clicking to show us their approval of our children, our beliefs, our politics, or even the mundane happenings of our daily lives. We engage in an unspoken social contract with others, agreeing to affirm them if they will affirm us in return. We desire fame. God desires faithfulness. He, alone, is, ultimately, worthy of our affirmation and adulation, having created all things (Revelation 4:11). May we long to be faithful, not famous, with our days.

PRAYER Father, I admit that I often long for my little slice of fame. I desire the applause and affirmation of those around me. You, however, are truly worthy of that applause. It is you, my creator and savior, that should get the standing ovation. Remind me of that truth, of the work of Jesus, that I might arrange my life to be one of faith and not fame. You, Lord, are the famous one. May my life do nothing less than make you known, to show your light in a dark and dying world. Amen.

Day 23

Psalm 116:12-14

12 What shall I return to the Lord
   for all his goodness to me?
13 I will lift up the cup of salvation
   and call on the name of the Lord.
14 I will fulfill my vows to the Lord
   in the presence of all his people.

OUR BEST There is a difficult realization imbedded in the idea that our response to God is to give Him our best, to offer Him every moment as a living sacrifice (Romans 12:1). Our best efforts and greatest days, while worshipful, are as filthy rags at the feet of our great King (Isaiah 64:6). And yet, like a child presenting well-intentioned art-work to a parent, our gift to God is not loved because of its excellence but its intent. We are His children, presenting a life akin to an outside-the-lines coloring page. While a slave may be judged according to his pro-duction, Scripture says we are adopted children, wholly acceptable because of our relationship (Galatians 4:7). We, therefore, have a Father who can accept our outside-the-lines lives and, in light of the work of

Jesus, receive them as a beautiful and pleasing offering.

PRAYER Good Father, thank you for choosing me, for adopting me. Thank you for searching me out in my loneliness and brokenness and loving me into your family. Thank you for sacrificing Jesus so that I, too, might be called your child. Your mercy is refreshing me every day and your grace gives me a life I could never have earned. Thank you. I love you. Amen.

Day 24

Psalm 116:12-14

12 What shall I return to the Lord
for all his goodness to me?
13 I will lift up the cup of salvation
and call on the name of the Lord.
14 I will fulfill my vows to the Lord
in the presence of all his people.

LIVE OUT LOUD What do we do when we experience something truly wonderful? We tell others! No matter the culture or age, to share that which we love is a universal trait of humanity. The psalmist is no exception. Spared from death and bathed in goodness and grace, David commits not only to fulfill his promises, but to do it in such a way that all will witness his life of gratitude. He is, in a sense, committing to *live out loud*, effectively turning his private response to the Lord into a public invitation so that others might know the goodness of God. What would it look like if we did the same?

PRAYER Lord, I fear that I have privatized you like everything else in our society. If I am honest, I keep quiet about you to avoid the rejection of those who don't yet know you or your love. Father, help my selfish insecurity and pride to die so I can proudly showcase the security I have found in you. Find me living out loud, displaying a life of grace and joy and eternal hope for all to see. Amen.

II LIFE TO GIVE II

Week 5: Psalm 116:15-19

15 Precious in the sight of the Lord
    is the death of his faithful servants.
16 Truly I am your servant, Lord;
    I serve you just as my mother did;
    you have freed me from my chains.
17 I will sacrifice a thank offering to you
    and call on the name of the Lord.
18 I will fulfill my vows to the Lord
    in the presence of all his people,
19 in the courts of the house of the Lord—
    in your midst, Jerusalem. Praise the
Lord.

One of the most rare and overwhelming experiences one can have is to see oneself clearly. Our society is painfully aware of (and even consumed with) self and yet true self-awareness is increasingly rare in modern culture. And it would seem that our personal pride rises in direct proportion to our waning self-awareness.

We are a people of pride, each living his or her Ptolemaic existence as the center of one's own universe. Only when we see ourselves as God sees us, glimpsing the humbling perspective of a universe that is not chiefly about us, do we break free from the me-centric lies of modern marketers and ease back into the God-centric reality of our design. True humility, as CS Lewis wrote, is not thinking less of yourself, but thinking of yourself less.

David found this freedom, recognizing that while God sees His creation as precious, it was not created for its own glory. What David has uncovered is a truth that resonates in our souls even as we grapple with trying to fully understand it. David's humble recognition that his life is a gift allows him, in beautiful and deferential meekness, to offer his life back to his Creator and rescuer. Oh, that we might find the same humility to clearly see our lives as such.

Day 25

Psalm 116:15-19

15 Precious in the sight of the Lord
   is the death of his faithful servants.
16 Truly I am your servant, Lord;
   I serve you just as my mother did;
   you have freed me from my chains.
17 I will sacrifice a thank offering to you
   and call on the name of the Lord.
18 I will fulfill my vows to the Lord
   in the presence of all his people,
19 in the courts of the house of the Lord—
   in your midst, Jerusalem. Praise the
Lord.

PRECIOUS CHILDREN Verse 15 seems morose at first reading, but the text is not indicating that God sees any death as precious as much as He sees the lives of the faithful as precious. The implication is that while all must die, the passing of the faithful, of God's adopted sons and daughters, does not go unnoticed. Rather, God sees each life as something of great value, something not to be wasted or treated trivially. This is a God who loves us deeply, who knows us intimately and personally

(Psalm 139:13). As we live a life pursuing meaning and significance in Him, we can rest assured knowing that He will not allow us to die in vain. We are God's precious children, created for a purpose and secured in eternity.

Prayer Father God, it is often hard for me to relate to you personally. I know you call me your child, but I still hold you as a distant dispensary of cosmic goodness. Forgive me. Grow my childlike trust and faith. Remind me that no matter how hard it is for me to relate to you, the incredible price you paid in choosing to relate to me - the life and death of Jesus - is evidence that you are a God who will stop at nothing to know me personally. Thank you for loving me that way, Father. Amen.

Day 26

Psalm 116:15-19

15 Precious in the sight of the Lord
    is the death of his faithful servants.
16 Truly I am your servant, Lord;
    I serve you just as my mother did;
    you have freed me from my chains.
17 I will sacrifice a thank offering to you
    and call on the name of the Lord.
18 I will fulfill my vows to the Lord
    in the presence of all his people,
19 in the courts of the house of the Lord—
    in your midst, Jerusalem. Praise the
Lord.

MEEKNESS Faithfulness and meekness
are inextricably linked. To be faithful to any-
thing other than oneself, we must be meek
enough to see that there is a way greater
than our own. To rest in the salvation of
God is to be meek enough to recognize that
we cannot save ourselves. David was re-
peatedly "brought low", allowing him to
clearly see his need for a delivering God
(Psalm 142:6). It is true that God works all
things to the good of those who love Him
(Romans 8:28) and that in our weakness

we most clearly see and feel the power of Christ (2 Corinthians 12:9). While no one desires to be brought low, to walk in suffering or trial, we can take heart that such experiences produce a humility and meekness that reminds us what a gracious and powerful God we serve.

Prayer Lord, you never waste my pain. When I cry, you answer. You know my sufferings and you experienced even greater trials through Jesus. Thank you for never abandoning me, for refusing to give up on me, and for pursuing me even in my sin. Thank you for choosing me to be your child. May I extend that relentless grace to those in my life who feel lost or abandoned, forsaken or beyond hope. May I be a real-life representative of your deep love. Amen.

Day 27

Psalm 116:15-19

15 Precious in the sight of the Lord
   is the death of his faithful servants.
16 Truly I am your servant, Lord;
   I serve you just as my mother did;
   you have freed me from my chains.
17 I will sacrifice a thank offering to you
   and call on the name of the Lord.
18 I will fulfill my vows to the Lord
   in the presence of all his people,
19 in the courts of the house of the Lord—
   in your midst, Jerusalem. Praise the
Lord.

FREED TO SERVE Everyone serves something. All of life is worship. Whether we live
our days for God or money, for material
possessions or worldly status, we all live for
something. We all serve something. Scripture tells us that we've been radically set
free, emancipated from the chains of sin
and made absolutely free in Christ. The
psalmist responds to God's rescue by
pledging a life of service back to God. Paul
tells the Romans that our freedom from
slavery to sin allows us to become slaves to

righteousness instead - willing volunteers in the fight for justice and goodness, ambassadors of light in a land of great darkness (Romans 6:15-23). What a joyful and meaningful calling!

Prayer Heavenly Father, I confess that I spend too many minutes and too many days silently worshipping something other than you. Father, show me how none of those false gods of money or significance or relationship will ever satisfy me. Remind my heart of the emptiness I knew before I knew you and draw me back to a life consumed by a love for you and a desire to do your will. Lord, let me be a blinding light of your grace in a world awash in darkness. Amen.

Day 28

Psalm 116:15-19

15 Precious in the sight of the Lord
   is the death of his faithful servants.
16 Truly I am your servant, Lord;
   I serve you just as my mother did;
   you have freed me from my chains.
17 I will sacrifice a thank offering to you
   and call on the name of the Lord.
18 I will fulfill my vows to the Lord
   in the presence of all his people,
19 in the courts of the house of the Lord—
   in your midst, Jerusalem. Praise the
Lord.

UNCHANGING TRUTH To serve the Lord
and fulfill our vows, it is implicit that we will
accept His truth. Our modern culture paints
an ever-moving target for truth, with the
only absolute truth being that truth is rela-
tive and will be changing again soon. To follow the Lord and His law is to be ridiculed
as old-fashioned, antiquated, ignorant, or
worse. And yet in the law we find comfort,
certainty, and unchanging truth (Psalm
119:51-56). What culture deemed acceptable in generations before is now scoffed

at. Truths that are championed today will be mocked tomorrow. The only way to stand firm today is to escape the shifting sands of society and stand firm on the rock, the unchanging and eternal truth of God's perfect law.

Prayer Lord, I am too-often concerned about the opinion of others. I scuffle in shifting sands trying to stay current with the times or trying to please people. In doing so, I abandon you and your teaching. And, yet, your law has never failed me. You have never let me down. Find me deeper in your truth, standing on the rock of your beautiful, unwavering goodness. Amen.

Day 29

Psalm 116:15-19

15 Precious in the sight of the Lord
   is the death of his faithful servants.
16 Truly I am your servant, Lord;
   I serve you just as my mother did;
   you have freed me from my chains.
17 I will sacrifice a thank offering to you
   and call on the name of the Lord.
18 I will fulfill my vows to the Lord
   in the presence of all his people,
19 in the courts of the house of the Lord—
   in your midst, Jerusalem. Praise the
Lord.

VOWS Biblically speaking, vows are debts
that must be paid. In the case of the
psalmist, he feels he "owes" for the salvation granted him from his persecutors and
from death itself. And yet, as Matthew Hen-
ry points out, it is better not to vow than to
vow and not pay. David's vow is a solemn
promise to live a life indebted to the goodness of God. As language in our modern
day slips into increasing informality through
a greater breadth of mediums than humanity has ever known, we would be wise to

take our own vows seriously. Our vows to each other matter and we will be held to account on them. Further, our vows to God are of great consequence. May we be steadfast in following the path He has laid out for us in Jesus.

Prayer Lord, I can be so flippant with language. Unwittingly, I confess that I have slipped into such irreverence with you, saying I will do one thing and living another way entirely. I long to be a child of obedience, Father. Give me the strength and endurance to hold fast to the vows I make. You paid my debt and gave me life. Let my vow be to return that life to you, worshipping you in all I do. Amen.

Day 30

Psalm 116:15-19

15 Precious in the sight of the Lord
  is the death of his faithful servants.
16 Truly I am your servant, Lord;
  I serve you just as my mother did;
  you have freed me from my chains.
17 I will sacrifice a thank offering to you
  and call on the name of the Lord.
18 I will fulfill my vows to the Lord
  in the presence of all his people,
19 in the courts of the house of the Lord—
  in your midst, Jerusalem. Praise the
Lord.

CULTIVATION OF GODLINESS David, in response to his rescue from danger and death, offers his life as a sacrifice. David speaks of the *courts of the house of the Lord.* In David's time, there was one altar, one place where God's people would gather and, in Calvin's words, "mutually stimulate one another to the cultivation of Godliness". The promise of the psalmist is not simply obedience, but a life poured out in encouragement of the righteousness and obedience of many. In the face of adversity, trial, and even death, our response is to be like that of David - a manifestation of inspiration, the Christ-life on display for the benefit of others and the glory of God. May we find our own gathering places to poor out our lives for the edification and encouragement of others. May our lives cultivate goodness, producing a harvest of deep righteousness that is pleasing to you and glorifying to your great name.

Prayer Father, what can I give back to you for the blessings you've poured out on me? May I live a life that is pleasing to you, a life of obedience that draws others to your altar. I recognize that every moment I have is a gift, a gracious allowance. Forgive me where I squander this life on meaningless trifles and vain pursuits. Find me, instead, running to your presence to offer you my whole self. May I seek that altar with every grace-soaked day I am given. Amen.

Psalm 116

1 I love the Lord, for he heard my voice; he heard my cry for mercy. 2 Because he turned his ear to me, I will call on him as long as I live. 3 The cords of death entangled me, the anguish of the grave came over me; I was overcome by distress and sorrow. 4 Then I called on the name of the Lord: "Lord, save me!" 5 The Lord is gracious and righteous; our God is full of compassion 6 The Lord protects the unwary; when I was brought low, he saved me. 7 Return to your rest, my soul, for the Lord has been good to you. 8 For you, Lord, have delivered me from death, my eyes from tears, my feet from stumbling, 9 that I may walk before the Lord in the land of the living. 10 I trusted in the Lord when I said, "I am greatly afflicted"; 11 in my alarm I said, "Everyone is a liar." 12 What shall I return to the Lord for all his goodness to me? 13 I will lift up the cup of salvation and call on the name of the Lord. 14 I will fulfill my vows to the Lord in the presence of all his people. 15 Precious in the sight of the Lord is the death of his faithful servants. 16 Truly I am your servant, Lord; I serve you just as my mother did; you have freed me from my *chains. **17** I will sacrifice a thank offering to you and call on the name of the Lord. **18** I will fulfill my vows to the Lord in the presence of all his people, **19** in the courts of the house of the Lord - in your midst, Jerusalem. Praise the Lord.*

Made in the USA
Lexington, KY
11 April 2017